THE CANADIAN BRASS
15 FAVORITE HYMNS

EASY ARRANGEMENTS

ARRANGED BY LARRY MOORE

Using the Arrangements
A music director/conductor can come up with various approaches to a hymn. For instance: verse 1 – no brass; verse 2 – brass (Standard Version); verse 3 – brass (Variation Verse); verse 4 – brass (Standard Version) with Trumpet Descant. Or, another example might be: verse 1 – brass (Standard Version) with keyboard; verse 2 – brass (Standard Version), no keyboard; verse 3 – brass (Variation Verse). Get creative!

Optional Trumpet Descant
The Conductor's Score also includes the part for a trumpet descant. The descant may be added to any of the Standard Version verses of a hymn. The trumpet part is available in the following Hal Leonard publication: 50485217 *The Canadian Brass: 15 Favorite Hymns–Trumpet Descants*

Visit the official website of The Canadian Brass:
www.canbrass.com

HAL•LEONARD®
CORPORATION
7777 W. BLUEMOUND RD. P.O. BOX 13819 MILWAUKEE, WI 53213

For all works contained herein:
Unauthorized copying, arranging, adapting, recording or public performance is an infringement of copyright.
Infringers are liable under the law.

Visit Hal Leonard Online at
www.halleonard.com

Tuba

ALL CREATURES OF OUR GOD AND KING

LASST UNS ERFREUEN

Francis of Assisi
Trans. W.H. Draper

Geistliche Kirchengesang
Harmonized by Ralph Vaughan Williams

STANDARD VERSION
Joyously (♩ = 120)

* *rit.* is used only if the Variation Verse is played as the final verse

Return to Standard Version as needed

Copyright © 2004 by HAL LEONARD CORPORATION
International Copyright Secured   All Rights Reserved

Tuba

CANADIAN BRASS
ALL GLORY, LAUD, AND HONOR
ST. THEODULPH

Theodulph of Orleans, ca. 820
Trans. by John Mason Neal, 1851; alt., 1859

Melchior Teschner, 1615

STANDARD VERSION
Regally (♩ = 108)

* *rit.* is used only if the Variation Verse is played as the final verse

Return to Standard Version as needed

Copyright © 2004 by HAL LEONARD CORPORATION
International Copyright Secured   All Rights Reserved

Tuba

CANADIAN BRASS
BLESSED ASSURANCE
ASSURANCE

Fanny J. Crosby

Phoebe P. Knapp

STANDARD VERSION
Spirited (♩. = 80)

Repeat as needed (opt.)

VARIATION VERSE

* *rit.* is used only if the Variation Verse is played as the final verse

Return to Standard Version as needed

Copyright © 2004 by HAL LEONARD CORPORATION
International Copyright Secured   All Rights Reserved

Tuba

CANADIAN BRASS

CHRIST THE LORD IS RISEN TODAY

EASTER HYMN

Charles Wesley

from *Lyra Davidica*, London, 1708

STANDARD VERSION
Joyously (♩ = 120)

Repeat as needed (opt.)

VARIATION VERSE

* *rit.* is used only if the Variation Verse is played as the final verse

Return to Standard Version as needed

Copyright © 2004 by HAL LEONARD CORPORATION
International Copyright Secured   All Rights Reserved

Tuba

CANADIAN BRASS

COME, YE THANKFUL PEOPLE, COME
ST. GEORGE'S, WINDSOR

Henry Alford

George J. Elvey

* *rit.* is used only if the Variation Verse is played as the final verse

Return to Standard Version as needed

Copyright © 2004 by HAL LEONARD CORPORATION
International Copyright Secured   All Rights Reserved

Tuba

CANADIAN BRASS
CROWN HIM WITH MANY CROWNS
DIADEMATA

Matthew Bridges, stanzas 1,2,4;
Godfrey Thring, stanza 3

George J. Elvey

STANDARD VERSION
Stately ($\quad$ = 112)

Repeat as needed (opt.)

Amen

VARIATION VERSE

rit. is used only if the Variation Verse is played as the final verse

Return to Standard Version as needed

Copyright © 2004 by HAL LEONARD CORPORATION
International Copyright Secured   All Rights Reserved

Tuba

CANADIAN BRASS

FAIREST LORD JESUS
(Beautiful Savior)
CRUSADERS' HYMN

Anonymous German Hymn, *Munster Gesangbuch*, 1677;
translated, Source unknown, stanzas 1-3; Joseph A. Seiss, Stanza 4

Schlesische Volkslieder, 1842
arranged by Richard S. Willis

STANDARD VERSION
Reverently (♩ = 84)

Repeat as needed (opt.)   Amen

VARIATION VERSE

Return to Standard Version as needed

Copyright © 2004 by HAL LEONARD CORPORATION
International Copyright Secured   All Rights Reserved

Tuba

CANADIAN BRASS
FOR THE BEAUTY OF THE EARTH
DIX

Folliott S. Pierpoint, altered

Conrad Cocher;
arranged by William H. Monk

STANDARD VERSION
Joyously (♩ = 120)

Repeat as needed (opt.)

Amen

VARIATION VERSE

3

rit. is used only if the Variation Verse is played as the final verse

Return to Standard Version as needed

Copyright © 2004 by HAL LEONARD CORPORATION
International Copyright Secured   All Rights Reserved

Tuba

CANADIAN BRASS
GOD OF OUR FATHERS
NATIONAL HYMN

Daniel C. Roberts

George W. Warren

* *rit.* is used only if the Variation Verse is played as the final verse

Return to Standard Version as needed

Copyright © 2004 by HAL LEONARD CORPORATION
International Copyright Secured   All Rights Reserved

Tuba

GUIDE ME, O THOU GREAT JEHOVAH
(God of Grace and God of Glory)
CWM RHONDDA

William Williams;
translated by Peter Williams

John Hughes

Repeat as needed (opt.)

Amen

VARIATION VERSE

(rit.)*

rit. is used only if the Variation Verse is played as the final verse

Return to Standard Version as needed

Copyright © 2004 by HAL LEONARD CORPORATION
International Copyright Secured   All Rights Reserved

CANADIAN BRASS

HOLY, HOLY, HOLY!
NICEA

Tuba

Reginald Heber

John B. Dykes

STANDARD VERSION
Reverently (♩ = 80)

mf

Repeat as needed (opt.)

Amen

VARIATION VERSE

(rit.)*

* *rit.* is used only if the Variation Verse is played as the final verse

Return to Standard Version as needed

Copyright © 2004 by HAL LEONARD CORPORATION
International Copyright Secured   All Rights Reserved

CANADIAN BRASS

JOYFUL, JOYFUL, WE ADORE THEE
HYMN TO JOY

enry van Dyke

Ludwig van Beethoven

STANDARD VERSION
Joyously (♩ = 132)

Repeat as needed (opt.)

Amen

VARIATION VERSE

(rit.)*

rit. is used only if the Variation Verse is played as the final verse

Return to Standard Version as needed

Copyright © 2004 by HAL LEONARD CORPORATION
International Copyright Secured   All Rights Reserved

Tuba

CANADIAN BRASS
LEAD ON, O KING ETERNAL
LANCASHIRE

Ernest W. Shurtleff

Henry T. Smart

STANDARD VERSION
Joyously (♩ = 120)

Repeat as needed (opt.)   Amen   VARIATION VERSE

(rit.)*

* *rit.* is used only if the Variation Verse is played as the final verse

Return to Standard Version as needed

Copyright © 2004 by HAL LEONARD CORPORATION
International Copyright Secured   All Rights Reserved

CANADIAN BRASS

Tuba

A MIGHTY FORTRESS IS OUR GOD

EIN FESTE BURG

Martin Luther
Trans. by F.H. Hedge, based on Psalm 46

Martin Luther

STANDARD VERSION
Steadily (♩ = 96)

* *rit.* is used only if the Variation Verse is played as the final verse

Return to Standard Version as needed

Copyright © 2004 by HAL LEONARD CORPORATION
International Copyright Secured   All Rights Reserved

Tuba

CANADIAN BRASS

O GOD, OUR HELP IN AGES PAST

ST. ANNE

Isaac Watts;
based on Psalm 90

attr. William Crof

STANDARD VERSION
Joyously (♩ = 100)

* *rit.* is used only if the Variation Verse is played as the final verse

Return to Standard Version as needed

Copyright © 2004 by HAL LEONARD CORPORATION
International Copyright Secured   All Rights Reserved